CW00672636

WHAT WE BURIED

Poems by Caitlyn Siehl

WORDS DANCE PUBLISHING
WordsDance.com

1st Edition
ISBN: 978-0615985862

Cover & Interior Design by Amanda Oaks

Words Dance Publishing
WordsDance.com

This is where we heal. This is where we hide. This is where we are found.

WHAT WE BURIED
Caitlyn Siehl

A LETTER TO LOVE

The first poem I wrote that wasn't about you
was in all capital letters,
like it was trying to compensate
for your absence.

It was about a world far away from this one,
where all of the plants were terrifying
but had healing powers, if you had the guts
to touch them.

The first poem I wrote that wasn't about you
puffed up its throat like a bullfrog
begging to be kissed.

It's my favorite poem because I hate it so much.

I read it at least once a day and think:
"So this is what I'm capable of without you. Go figure."

There is a hole in everything
and I find you there, smiling
like you don't have anywhere else to be.

The first poem I wrote that wasn't about you
might one day be regarded as a masterpiece.
People will come from all over the world
to run their fingers over the print
and marvel at how empty it is of you.

They will not recognize your scent
clinging silently to their hands.
Because if you walk into a room
and notice what is missing from it,
It's still there, isn't it?

The first poem I wrote that wasn't about you
was still about you.
Damn it.
Always.

THREE QUESTIONS

My mother tells me that, when I meet someone I like,
I have to ask them three questions:

1. What are you afraid of?
2. Do you like dogs?
3. What do you do when it rains?

Of those three, she says the first one is the most important.
*"They gotta be scared of something, baby. Everybody is. If they aren't afraid
of anything, then they don't believe in anything, either."*

I met you on a Sunday, right after church.
One look and my heart fell into my stomach
like a trap door.

On our second date, I asked you what you were afraid of.
*"Spiders, mostly. Being alone. Little children, like,
the ones who just learned how to push a kid over on the playground.
Oh and space. Holy shit, space."*

I asked you if you liked dogs.
"I have three."

I asked you what you do when it rains.
*"Sleep, mostly. Sometimes I sit at the window and watch the rain droplets
race. I make a shelter out of plastic in my backyard for all the stray animals;
Leave them food and a place to sleep."*

He smiled like he knew, like his mom told him the same thing.
"How about you?"

Me?
I'm scared of everything.

Of the hole in the o-zone layer, of the lady next door
who never smiles at her dog, and especially of all the secrets
the government must be breaking its back trying to keep from us.
I love dogs so much, you have no idea.

I sleep when it rains.
I want to tell everyone I love them.
I want to find every stray animal and bring them home.
I want to wake up in your hair and make you shitty coffee
and kiss your neck and draw silly stick figures of us.
I never want to ask anyone else these questions ever again.

IN THE LAND OF THE LIVING

In the world where we are together,
the rivers have hands that pray.
The birds have learned how to cry
and worms have hearts and a central nervous system.

Everything is human here.

Spiders pay rent to stay in the corners of our ceilings.
Trees sing folk songs about their fallen brothers and sisters.
The wind is their mother swaying them to sleep, trying to
quiet the grief.

The rocks write poems about the ocean
but never show them to her.
They cry erosion and she does not know
how to give back what she has taken.

I kiss you in front of the bruised face of the moon
and can hear the blood pooling
underneath her silver skin.

There is no shame here.

The grass begs for our bodies and we oblige.
The crickets tune their strings and start playing their symphony.
We are never alone, but we are free.
The earth has a pulse that we check with our bare feet.
Even the concrete hums.

LIKE THE TREES

In this world, with trees that have seen my great grandfather
grow old and die, we dance like fevers.

I rest my hand on your neck and I feel the life brimming
at the tip of your spine. I press my lips to the vein
in the crook of your elbow. There is not enough time
to love you like the trees.

I want to spend a decade on just your hands,
until I can tell yours apart from someone else's
just by brushing past them.

I want to spend a century on your mouth,
until I can taste you just by breathing near you.

In this land of ivy and weeds, of living, beating things,
I want to grow until the sky has to expand
to make room for me.

I want to know you like the river under my skin.
I want our roots to make the earth weep.

THE ARCHITECT

I could build cities on the earth in your eyes
if you let my hands draw the landscape
of your jawbone and trace the river
that runs down your cheeks
and splays into a delta
in the pools of your collarbones.
I didn't go to school for this
but when I saw your face
I wondered if architecture
was sleeping latent in my bones.
I wondered if I was born to know
the blueprints of you.

I AM NOT AFRAID OF YOU

Bring me your malice,
your angry, your spiteful.
Tie them in a knot tightly
and leave them at my door.
Bring me your drunk,
your stubborn,
your clenched fist
and I will bring you mine.
Bring me your impatience,
your stranger, your ghosts.
Wring out the silent screams
soaking your pillow.
Bring them to me.
Bring them all to me.
You do not have to repent
for the parts of you that
don't see the daylight.
You do not have to burn
your old self to the ground
just to make room for me.
Bring me your bad, your worst,
your loneliest. I will kiss them each
where it hurts. If it does not help,
I will turn the other cheek.
I will put out the fire.
Bring me your rickety bridge,
your 400 foot fall if it breaks.
I am not afraid of you.
I am not afraid of you.
I am not afraid of you.

KINDLING

I am all mouth, with teeth like kindling.
Do not kiss me before you know this.
I am all hunger, all restraint and poised bones,
coiled spine, patient spring.

The mouse traps in my grandmother's basement
look like my hands, and I'm telling you this because
I am no better than the stories you've heard.
I am no softer than the feast of skin on your neck
or the valleys behind your kneecaps.

Do you taste the way my name sounds?
Do you hear the apology I whispered
into the cave of your collarbone?

I am still learning how to ask
the important questions, like
"Do you want children?" or
"How do you take your coffee?"
so I'm sorry if I stare at your mouth
and ask you if you've ever swallowed
a dandelion seed, instead.

The ones who came before you
will tell you that I am their tragedy,
their burning building,
but that is only because
they didn't
understand.

This poem is not for them, anyway.

Don't be alarmed if you taste smoke
after you whisper that you love me
through my lips, okay?

That just means I heard you.

REMEMBERING

You watch me when I put my lipstick on,
say you can tell how I'm going to tell you I love you
by the color I choose.

Pink is all hands.
Plum is marks on your neck and a poem.
Red is straight back and a steady voice.

For a brief moment, I wonder if it should be this easy.
If people are allowed to know each other
from the lipstick they wear
down to the way their fingers twitch
when they're about to cry.

I can't remember ever not loving you.
I try, but all I feel is cold tile under my hands,
and then your back.

I think about how strong humans are,
yet, if I fall on my spine
the wrong way,
I'll never feel your hands on me again.

Today, my mouth is your favorite fruit.
I am writing you this poem to tell you
that I asked my sister if she broke her teeth
when she fell in love. I asked her if it was okay
that it didn't happen that way, for me.

I did not fall in love with you,
I was born on the floor.
Everything else was just remembering.

MYTHOLOGY

She holds her hair up with only
two chopsticks and a bobby pin.
Think Atlas. Think shoulders.
When your sadness starts to feast,
she carries the light down from the
mountain and hands it to you,
tells you to set it on fire.
Think Prometheus. Think savior.
On Sunday, she steps out of the shower
and you don't think you've ever seen
anything more beautiful than the way
she walks towards you with a towel
on her head, water clinging to her
like there is nowhere else it would rather be.
Think Aphrodite. Think sea foam.
You love her like mythology.
You love her like the impossible stories
of Gods and monsters.
When she sings, think fairies.
Think mermaids. Think hymns.
She is the face of the river
that Narcissus fell in love with,
confusing hers for his own.
She is Medusa's fury,
Athena's strength,
Achelois' healing.
You are kissing her in a crowded
restaurant and it feels like praying.
You are watching her
instead of the meteor shower
and you don't even notice.

BREAKFAST

You are stirring from your sleep
like cream in coffee, going from dark
to light to warm when I press my mouth
to your mouth.

I always wake up before you, just for this moment.
You are better than caffeine because I can kiss you
on an empty stomach and not feel sick.
My hands still shake, but that's because
there's a piano getting tuned in my palms,
strings vibrating, trying to find the exact key
your skin is written in.

You are the reason I hum with my mouth full.
You are the reason music makes me weep.
I can't write about you without writing
about the morning because that is the time
I love you best. Over eggs and bacon.

You yawn and I hear cellos.
You blink and I hear drums.

There are birds outside the window
begging for me to shut up but I can't stop
singing along to the symphony of your body
when it is just waking up.

I love you best over breakfast.
You groan when you burn your tongue
on your coffee and I swear I've never heard
a more beautiful sound.

DESPERATE

We kissed because we were starving for it.
We were so desperate with each other
that every time we went out, at least one person
would pull me to the side and ask if one of us
was dying. The answer, of course, was always yes.
We didn't even know what to do with our hands.
Sometimes, they'd wind up on my mouth,
over your entire face, trailing up and down
your spine, nails like rakes over angry red skin.
It couldn't have been pretty, and God,
if you were watching, you're a pervert,
but I'm also sorry. We loved like we were
trying to make up for lost time.
Every touch an apology, an
"I'm sorry I haven't been with you every day since elementary school."
There was no way it wouldn't end badly,
so we stayed away from fire, because we knew
what it could do to beautiful things.
We spent an hour every day in separate parts
of the apartment, relearning distance, trying
to remember how to measure in feet and inches
instead of eyelashes and arms.
I could feel you in the kitchen.
I could feel how tense your muscles were,
how tightly your jaw was clenched.
Every length of you was humming without me.
I knew you like the back of your hand.
Every vein, every freckle. That scar in-between
your middle and ring finger from when you
fell down during a game of kickball.
It was all urgency, all fire-engine red.
We saw the smoke coming from a mile away
and kissed the treetops before they coughed
and writhed under the flames.
It was a beautiful forest. Too beautiful to stay.
I will never forget the place that I loved you,
even if it is raining ash. I hear some of the trees
are still alive on the inside.

WHAT I'LL TELL THEM

I promise not to love you like an after school special
and that my kisses will always be barbaric.
At night, I will bare my neck to the sword of your tongue,
to the punishment of your teeth.
I will wear the marks like a necklace
as people stare at your lip, bitten raw.
My mom tells me that I watch too much
television, so my idea of love is all smooth skin
and 5 minute commercials when I get tired,
but not here. Not you. I will eat your sighs
and harvest them in my belly until winter,
until they ripen the shape of my name.
I will press my hands into the wet
cement of your ribcage until
you can see fingerprints.
I will learn your anger. I will lick your sadness.
I will feast on your hunger.
I promise a banquet for our ending.
I promise a parade of drums for the day you
close the door behind you for the last time.
I promise not to carry you around with me like a mistake
or a pack of gum, even when I forget what you taste like.
When they ask me about you,
I will always smile.
I will say your name and it will sound
like *"thank you."*

DO NOT FALL IN LOVE WITH PEOPLE LIKE ME

Do not fall in love with people like me.
People like me will love you so hard
that you turn into stone,
into a statue where people come to marvel at how long
it must have taken to carve that faraway look into your eyes.

Do not fall in love with people like me.
We will take you to museums and parks and monuments
and kiss you in every beautiful place
so that you can never go back to them
without tasting us like blood in your mouth.

Do not come any closer.
People like me are bombs.
When our time is up, we will splatter loss all over your walls
in angry colors that make you wish your doorway
never learned our name.

Do not fall in love with people like me.
With the lonely ones.
We will forget our own names if it means learning yours.
We will make you think that hurricanes are gentle,
that pain is a gift.

You will get lost in the desperation, in the longing
for something that is always reaching,
but never able to hold.

Do not fall in love with people like me.
We will destroy your apartment.
We will throw apologies at you that shatter on the floor
and cut your feet.

We will never learn how to be soft.
We will leave.
We always do.

SMALL THINGS

We will lose each other in the small things,
like which movie to watch
or how much cream we put in our coffee.

I will stop singing
and you will stop noticing.

Our city will crumble so slowly
that we won't feel it
until the kitchen is covered in dust
and we don't dance in it anymore.

The truth is,
I saw this coming from a state away.

Just outside of Pennsylvania,
a house fire screamed angry
as fire trucks tried to save it,
and I knew it was over
when you kissed me after we passed it.

We will lose each other in the small things.

I will start washing the ash off of my hands
after I touch you and you'll pretend that
falling asleep on the couch night after night
is an accident.

It's not that I don't love you,
it's just that I can't pretend like the roof isn't caving in
or that I don't see the smoke leaking out
from the gaps in your teeth.

Forgive me, darling,
but I cannot walk into the place
that is burning.
I am already on fire
and I cannot save you.

THE MURAL

You are the mistakes I made in college.
You are the eighth shot of Southern Comfort
and the walk back to my dorm that I don't remember.
If I'm being honest, I miss being that reckless.
Your neck is a mural of lips that belonged to women
who never loved you and I refuse to be one of them.
You are a hangover.
You are breakfast at 3 in the afternoon.
You make me sick and I love you.
I will not kiss your neck with imperfect courage.
I will cover their lips with my own
and I will never be embarrassed
about throwing up in my own hair
that night I called you and told you
that you were the worst miracle I'd ever known,
because I meant terrifying.
I meant perfect.
I meant please don't leave,
I'm trying to make this a good thing,
and you knew.
You knew.

QUESTIONS FOR A FEW YEARS FROM NOW

Do you love with your mouth closed or open?
Do you taste chocolate or licorice when you kiss them?
When you see them, which hand reaches for them first?
Do you love with the blinds open?
In the daytime?
When no one is watching?
How many times a day do your feet tap the rhythm of their name?
Where do you like to fuck?
Where do you like to make love?
Is there a difference?
If so, what shade is it?
Do you still take your coffee black?
How long has it been since you smoked?
Do they make it easier to breathe
or do you still use your inhaler?
When was the last time you unlocked the liquor cabinet?
When you slow dance, are your eyes open or closed?
Do they smell like your sheets when you leave for work?
What does their sadness sound like?
Trumpets? A wolf howl?
Do they make you happier than I did?
Don't answer.
Don't answer.
Don't answer.

BEND THE LIGHT

All of my poems are about the same thing and it's your fault.
Teeth and hands, something about forgetting, eventually,
and then the sky. Always the sky.
I wonder why I bother with writing at all.
I can't drink coffee anymore because it makes me throw up
and I'm pretty sure at least half of me is dying.
Where have you been?
This poem is not for you, but maybe it is.
Last time I saw you I made it a point not to touch you,
and this all could have turned out differently if I had,
but I can't worry about that now.
You are beyond a song stuck in my head.
You are the reason I tie my hair in knots
and why my parents think I'm crazy.
Apparently black holes can bend light when they pass through it,
so now I'm wondering if you have one resting chaotic in your belly,
because I am twisted like metal in a car crash
just thinking about you touching me.
I can't decide if this poem is angry or pathetic
or something entirely different.
All I know is I spend too much time
imagining your fingers and how they would flutter
while you play the piano.
Sometimes I pretend my spine is a keyboard,
and you run a scale up my back,
just to see if I'm in tune.
My world is so full of you that
the hum of the ocean even sounds like your name.
One day, it will be better.
I will put the pen down
and forget how to remember the nights I tried
to write you out of my system like an addiction.
It will be remarkable and I'll still want to call you.

REMEMBER

Do not think, remember.
My mouth, your mouth,
crushing grapes between our teeth
and drinking the wine.
The red dripping down our chins like blood.
Do not think, remember.
The rain in the window.
The daddy longlegs crawling like a raindrop
down to the floor. Your head in my lap,
hair sprawled like roots across my snow thighs.
Remember. Remember.
Our hands, always our hands,
poking holes into each other like train tickets.
You standing on the platform,
just past the yellow line,
waving, waving, waving, unsure
if it was hello or goodbye. Remember.
Quick and fast movements in the dark
before the sun came up and we had
beaten each other tender.
A pile of intertwined limbs on the mattress,
breathing softly.
Do not think, remember.
My toes. My ears. My freckles.
Each place you tucked yourself away
and waited for me to find you.
My elbows. The valley in between my thumb
and pointer finger. My hips. My tongue.
Remember how we were two people,
discovering each other for the first time.
How we got lost in the parts of each other
that went too deep.
How we clawed our way out.
How we wanted to go back.
How we couldn't.
How every other place feels like hiding now.
Do not think, remember.
Remember me.

THE PARK

This is where we laid like children in the grass
and sang purple bruises into the sky
until it was night.

When I walk the dog, I come here.
I stand where we stood and I do not cry.
I watch the geese watch me with indifference
and I love them.

I watch the grass weep and bend in the wind
and I understand what it is like
to be such a small, growing thing.
Sometimes, we have to leave.
I do not miss you, but sometimes
that isn't true. Mostly I hear you,
and that is different.

I go to the park with all the empty benches
and run my fingers along the initials
carved like promises into damp wood.

I loved you, I did. I loved you as good as anybody,
and I'll never be sorry.

This is the place I finally learned what it meant
to dance alone to the song you put in my chest.

Thanks for the symphony.

I can still hear it when I think of you,
and it is so much like remembering.

THIS IS NOT A LOVE POEM

I cannot tell you how longs it's been
since I thought about kissing you.
No, no, no. I promise this isn't a love poem,
just let me say this.
I cannot tell you how long it's been
since I wanted to call you and pretend
it was an accident,
or text you and ask you a question
that I already knew the answer to.
I stopped counting after 6 months
and never looked back, except
on really, really bad days, when I needed
something to hurt so I pretended
you loved me but you were just bad at showing it.
I grew my bangs out because I can't
stop picking my nails when they get
too long and I wanted to be able
to tuck them behind my ears
like a pencil or a bad joke that I could use later.
I dyed my hair a darker shade of brown
and tell people it's just the weather
that makes me look so pale because it's probably true.
What I'm trying to say is that I don't
think about you anymore when
I do my makeup and drive around,
even when it's snowing and I can't
stop talking about the northern lights.
A year ago, I would have crushed a bunch
of beer bottles and thrown them
into the sunlight and called the sparkle good enough,
but now I don't even wish that you were here to see this.
I mean, I hope you're happy,
but the sky is still the sky without you,
and I'm not surprised by that anymore.

UNREQUITED

I was 19 when I finally stopped opening the door
for unrequited love.
I was 20 when I first learned that courage
tasted like bitter wine and metal.
Like blood and honey.
When I told you I loved you, I screamed it.
I let it rip its way out of my throat,
and it felt so good that I cried.
The other day,
you walked by me with your friends
and I could feel the pity in your stare.
Don't you do that.
Don't you look at what I had for you and call it weak.
Not when you were the one afraid of it.
I stood there with my hands open,
my mouth bruised tender with supplication.
Don't you dare treat me like a victim
of my own emotions,
like being moved to my knees by love
was a mistake that I regret.
I will go to my grave with the memory
of the bravery in my bones.
I am not ashamed of any of it.
Not the closed door in my face
or the static silence of my phone
for weeks after.
I was not afraid.
I am still not afraid.
I will never be afraid again.
Bring in the beasts with teeth like tree branches.
Bring in all the men who will never love me.
Bring in the monsters with faces carved out of stone.
I am not afraid.
They can eat me alive.
I am not afraid.
I will cut my way out of their bellies.
I am not afraid.
Never again.

STRETCH MARKS

I learned how to be big by accident.
I was 10 and I didn't look like the other girls.
I was 10 and it was too late to turn back.
The kids had already learned how to
wield the knives under their tongues
so I kept quiet when they spat.
I stayed soft and I forgave.

The first few popped up on my inner thigh
when I turned fourteen, splaying out like
white trees on smooth skin.

When I told my friends, they did not look proud.
I learned how to be big by accident.

A patch reached across my hips when I turned 16 and
the white rivers opened up into a delta on my calves.
I was a landscape.
I was art.

I kept growing and they kept coming like refugees
from some falling country.
"Give me your tired, your poor."

I am a city of sounds.
I will keep you safe.

I know I am supposed to feel ugly.
They all tell me that no woman
should look so well-traveled,
but they do not know.

I am earth. I am sun and skies.
I am the high road, the low road.
I am every poem about skin.
I am a world that cannot be explored in one day.
I am not a place for cowards.

FUNNY GIRL
After Megan Falley

I tell myself: Be a funny girl, baby.
Don't let them see you without a smile.
I tell myself: Don't be boring, baby.
They'll never stop teasing you
if you don't make them laugh.
Fat girl.
I tell myself I can be a funny girl, instead.
Funny girl can make people forget.
I tell myself: Don't you dare be sad in front of them.
Don't you dare cry.
I tell myself not to fall in love
with the first boy who likes my poetry.
I tell myself not to fall in love
with the first boy who doesn't like my jokes.
Funny girl, he can see how serious you are.
I tell myself not to fall in love with the first boy
who doesn't ask me to make him laugh.
Funny girl isn't a clown, I think.
Don't fall in love because it's been so long, baby.
Don't fall in love because he likes it when you cry.
I tell myself to be careful.
Funny girl is running out of punch-lines
and she is using her own jaw instead.
Funny girl is dying with a smile,
swallowing down a panic attack
when she has to squeeze into a seat on the bus.
I tell myself: No one can hurt you if you hurt yourself, first.
They will be too busy helping you clean up the mess.
I tell myself: You don't have to wear this armor if it is too heavy.
You don't have to be afraid of your silence.
Funny girl, you are so much more than what
you've let yourself become.
You are not a circus, okay?
You are not a circus.
You are not a circus.

GIRL

Girl, bite. Girl, devour. Girl, don't forgive.
Girl, stay angry. Girl, be selfish.
Girl, walk away from him when he raises his hand.
There is no place that can handle you,
but you must go anyway, to the hills, the mountains, the cities.
They'll call you monster, and they'll be so right.
Girl, show them.
Girl, run your hands along the wound and seal it with your heat.
Cauterize.
They thought they could get to you.
They thought they could take you and make you small.
There may be bruises, but you are no little thing.
Girl, show them your claws.
Show them your wings.
Rise.
Show them your army of injuries who have come to fight.
Show them the others like you.
Take over the city. Own the mountains.
Bite the hand and the one behind their back with all the good stuff.
Girl, show your teeth.
Never forget what you can do with them.

PREY

Here is the ending before the beginning.
I pick you out of my teeth like spinach.
I take a bath and I don't think about drowning myself.
My sister spends the weekend at the apartment
and doesn't ask me about it, even though she can see
that my teeth have gotten sharper since last time.
Your name is just a name.
I am still in one piece when I close the door.
I say *"thank you for everything"* and wipe my mouth.
You watch the Discovery Channel
and see a lioness lick her bloody paws after a kill.
You think of me and wonder if the grass
was really so tall that you couldn't see me coming.
I am growing into something fierce and hungry.
When I kiss your skin, I am only trying to taste your bones.
Whatever is left of you, I hope it forgets me.

SKY POEM

Consider the stars.
That is always the first thing I say
when I want to write a poem.
Do not forget about the sky.
This is how it goes.
Everything I write is a love letter
to things that can't be touched.
Last Tuesday, I made sure
not to brush hands with the man
who handed me my coffee because
I knew I'd spend the next week
stuck on his fingers, like a fool.
Consider the moon.
I cry if I sit still for too long
because my body can't think
of any other way
to remind itself that it isn't dying.
The moon doesn't like me very much.
I've seen the way she scowls at me when I sing.
This is all new. This is all so ancient.
I don't know how I've found the language for it.
I am writing this poem to remember everything
that is bigger and more brutal than me.
Stars are not small or gentle.
They are writhing and dying and burning.
They are not here to be pretty.
I am trying to learn from them.

CIRCUS TRICKS

This is for the mornings I wake up wanting
to crush my teeth into gunpowder.
This is reminder, warning, promise.
I am going to be angry, and because
I was never taught to embrace it,
I will hold it in, like a good girl.
Because a bloody fist is not poetry on me,
but I can write about it when I think of him
and his fury and the hole in the wall
and how gorgeous it looked when he wore my rage.
I welcomed his hate inside of me
because mine needed company.
My venom is different than his.
Mine swims like a snake through my veins
and I have learned how to sing it
into silence.
His is always screaming.
His is always tragic.
Never crazy, never unlovable, always forgiven.
This is for the mornings I wake up
and taste something burning on my tongue.
This is for when I kick him out.
This is for when I reach into my throat
and pull out the match, careful not to strike it
against my teeth.
This is for me.
This is for when I call my mom
and talk about the first time she took me
to the circus, how I couldn't keep my eyes
off of the man breathing fire.

"Doesn't that hurt him, mama?"

*"No, baby, he's been practicing his whole life.
Look how pretty it is when he spits it out."*

IN THIS STORY

In this story, your mother isn't the villain.
In this story, you find a way to pick the lock,
to wake up, to climb out of the tower yourself.
In this story, you're angry.
In this story, you meet a dragon and it is afraid of you.
In this story, you don't need to be saved.
In this story, your mother raised you to recognize a prison
from a home.
In this story, they don't fall in love with you before they know you.
In this story, they aren't better than you.
In this story, you have claws.
In this story, happily ever after has bite marks in it.
In this story, you are free and terrifying.
In this story, you get away.
In this story, you bleed.
In this story, you survive.

MAYBE EVE WAS A WILD THING

Tell them you don't know how Eve felt
when the snake brought you his heart like an apple
and your thirst, your hunger, your curiosity
all red and pulsating like an open wound, made you take it
and hold it until your knees gave out, until he carried you
into the darkness like some white horse who mistook
the street lights for a sunset.

Tell them you don't know how Eve felt the morning after,
when the skies parted and you realized that all angels
are demons who haven't been cast out yet,
so you ask him to stay and he does,
and you look at him, that man,
the one with the empty chest, the one
everyone warned you about, and he may not be God,
but at least he's here.

Oh, Eden is so sweet. Eden is so beautiful,
but you do not want to stay here forever.

Tell them you don't know how Eve felt
when she was told that she was the downfall of humankind
before humankind even began. When eating that apple
made her the first wild thing, the first beautiful creature
to not do as they're told.

Your heart is an offering, not a caged bird.
This man in your bed may be a mistake,
he may answer the questions you didn't want to know,
but you will grow. Your roots will spread across the seas,
your limbs growing apples, your heart growing thorns
to protect itself.

Tell them you don't know how Eve felt
when she saw Adam in one hand,
and the rest of the universe in the other.

Tell them you don't know how Eve felt
when she wanted the universe.

WHEN THE BOYS COME

When the boys pull your hair and push you to the ground
during recess, I promise not to tell you that it's because
they like you. When the teachers call home to tell me
that you pushed them to the ground after you,
I'll take you out of school early and buy you
your favorite ice cream.

When you get older and the boys try to touch you
when you don't want to be touched,
I'll look at you like the sun when you come home
with anger in your fists.

They all tell you not to fight fire with fire,
but that is only because they are afraid of your flames.

When the boys yell after you like hyenas, you yell back, baby.
I will not teach you to be afraid of your anger
so that you look for it in others.
I will not make you be the better person,
because you already are.
You wanna fight 'em? Fight 'em.
Don't you dare apologize for the fierce love
you have for yourself
and the lengths you go to preserve it.

When the boys try to tell you to soften up,
I hope you make them bleed with your edges.
I hope you remember that you are not theirs,
that their disappointment in you is not yours.
When the boys come to your door with pretty words
and angry eyes, I hope you show them the anger in yours.
I hope you show them just how strong your mommy thinks you are.
I hope you show them the animal they can't always see
in their own reflection.

When the boys come with the intention of hurting you,
my advice will always stay the same, my darling:
Give 'em hell.

IT IS NOT YOUR JOB

When your little girl asks you if she's pretty,
your heart will drop like a wineglass on the hardwood floor.
Part of you will want to say
"Of course you are, don't ever question it,"
and the other part, the part that is clawing at you,
will want to grab her by her shoulders,
look straight into the wells of her eyes
until they echo back to you and say
"You do not have to be if you don't want to. It is not your job."
Both will feel right.
One will feel better.
She will only understand the first.
When she wants to cut her hair off
or wear her brother's clothes,
you will feel the words in your mouth like marbles.
"You do not have to be pretty if you don't want to.
It is not your job."

THE FIRST WORD I TEACH MY DAUGHTER

The first word I teach my daughter will be *"No."*
She will sing it to me and scream it at me
and I will never tell her to quiet down.
She will say it when I tell her to go to bed,
when I tell her she can't have any more candy
or watch any more television.
"No" will be my daughter's favorite word.
Not only will I teach her how to say it,
but I will teach her to repeat it over and over
again until every single atom in her tiny little body hums with it.
If it makes her less soft than the other girls,
I will take her to museums and show her
what marble and stone can become.
I will brush her hair and let her wear whatever she wants.
If this makes her a warrior in a field of flowers,
then she will walk without fear of being trampled on.
The first word I teach my daughter will be *"No"*
and when she grows up in a world that tells her
that she can't walk down the street by herself,
that *"No"* will be heard.
It will roar and echo down the block
and she will never be told to keep silent.
She will not know the meaning of the word.

A LETTER TO MY FUTURE SON

If you ever want to wear mommy's make-up,
just make sure you don't eat it.
When it's time to go to bed, I will help you wash it off.
When school starts and you want to jump rope
instead of play kickball, be careful not to trip
and hurt your knees. If you grow up and a boy
makes your heart hurt, you do not have to
be ashamed. If you fall in love with a girl
who wears the same clothes as you,
it will be easy for me to buy you both presents.
If I teach you anything, I will teach you to be gentle.
You are not Atlas and the world is not a burden for you to carry.
If you do not like your body, if you feel like you were put inside
the wrong one, I will stand by and watch you become again.
Because we are human beings and we do not always have to
take what we are given.
I will love you constantly, fervently, always.
I will teach you the value of the word *"no"* so that,
when you hear it, you do not question it.
When the war comes and you want to fight,
I will sleep with clenched fists until you come home to me.
When the war comes and you don't want to go,
I will sleep soundly.
You are allowed to be soft.
You are allowed to break and bend.
You do not have to be strong.
You do not have to be a soldier.

FOR THE DINNER TABLE

For the dinner table.
For the men who have made you
believe that you are some place that can be left.
You move like a thief in a jewelry store,
always poised for an alarm, for
a mistake, and I don't know how
to tell you that the diamonds are already yours.
For the coffee mug with your name on it.
For the yoga mat in the closet
that is forgetting your hands.
I want to be with you in the place where you
have not made yourself small,
in the place where you still love my poetry
and don't smile like surrender.
For the home in your throat.
For your ankles.
For the prayer in your teeth.
I love you like freedom.
I love you like there is no room for anything else.
I love you like straight spine.
I just wish you would stand up
and meet me there.

THE MANTRA

When you met Atlas, he almost dropped the world
just to shake your hand.
The first man who wasn't afraid of you
and he couldn't even hold you.
Misery is at its best when no one is around.
It dances with you at night and tucks you in
when morning comes.
There are bruised bottles hugging your floor,
begging for you not to kiss them again because
they are so empty, and maybe this time,
you won't go looking for more.
When the world ends, I think it will start at the center.
I think it will start with a whisper and then reach
through the soil to grab at our ankles.
I think that, when this happens, you will kick
its shrieking fingers into submission.
You will look at the end and tell it to keep going.
There will be no pity or doubt in your voice
when you will the world to keep humming,
because how many times have you been through this?
How many times have you kept the agony at bay?
I want to hear you say it,
you sinker of stones, you river of tomorrows,
you monument of sorrow,
you forest of fireworks:
I am allowed to be here, even if sometimes
it feels like a punishment.
I am the core of the earth,
and I am burning so beautifully.

SURVIVAL

This is how we survive:
We survive.
I have learned that there aren't tricks
for breaking the fingers
of the things that choke us in our sleep.
There aren't remedies that take away
heartache without the word "time"
written sympathetically across our therapist's face.
We survive by surviving.
We do it unconsciously,
the way our bodies remember to
breathe, even when we're asleep.
The first step is always deciding
to take the first step.
The second step is miserable
and we usually trip down the stairs,
then wait months before climbing back
and starting again.
What I'm trying to say is, be patient.
What I'm trying to say is, I don't have the answers.
My bones tell me to sing when I'm lonely, so I do.
I sing and I don't think of him or his hands.
On days when everything feels
like a eulogy, walk slowly, and don't wear black.
Don't let this be a funeral.
Teach yourself to navigate the wound
and take note of all the places
you see along the way, like the park bench
with your initials carved into it,
or the weeping willow that is tired of crying.
There will be months that try to swallow
you whole, with fangs that pierce your chest
like a bullet. Look for the exit wound.
Look for the Hallelujah chorus
at the other end of your skin.
It has come and gone and now everything
is a symphony.

THE POET

The poet chews on tree bark and tastes centuries of fire.
The poet writes about this for four weeks while barely sleeping.
It is raining broken glass and the poet sticks their tongue out,
surrendering to the shards and the bright red roses that bloom
like metal in their mouth.

The poet waits for the weather to change, and, in the meantime,
falls in love with a walking wound so bright and beautiful that they
do not feel the gash in their chest when they leave.

The poet collects the winter in the cut and keeps it there to thaw
by the fireplace. The poet watches the snow fall over the body of a
dead deer like a blanket and wonders if nature is just trying its best.

The poet eats the spring like an appetizer and it won't stop raining
in the place where their ribs stop linking fingers.

Loss is a universal language.

The earth is bleeding somewhere with quiet sincerity, and the poet
cannot find where it is coming from.

Summer is an ugly bruise that won't stop yellowing,
so the poet does not write, but swims to soothe the ache.
It feels more like waiting.

Fall comes, and the poet thinks about eating a star.
The poet thinks about carrying the moon around with them
like a balloon.

The poet thinks about the sun being understood.
It would be a mistake to write about anything else.

Caitlyn is primarily interested in healing. Growing up in a small town in New Jersey, she began writing poetry three years ago with the intention of bringing pain to the surface, of clawing through the dirt and excavating it before singing it to sleep. She tries to be gentle with what hurts, and it has helped.

Currently a student at Rutgers University, Caitlyn is studying film and journalism in the hopes of becoming a screenwriter.

At twenty-years-old, she is still growing. She has found her voice and it is a delicate thing, so she is happy to be sharing it.

LITERARY SEXTS
a collection of short & sexy love poems

Edited by Amanda Oaks & Caitlyn Siehl, hovering around 50 contributors & 125 poems, this book reads is like one long & very intense conversation between two lovers. It's absolutely breathtaking.

These are poems that you would text to your lover. Poems that you would slip into a back pocket, suitcase, wallet or purse on the sly. Poems that you would write on slips of paper & stick under your crush's windshield wiper. Poems that you would write on a Post-it note & leave on the bathroom mirror. Treat yourself, a crush or a lover with this lush gift!

My body intends
to be seen.

My body intends
to shine.

My fat is not quiet.

My fat sparkles.

SPARKLEFAT
Poetry by Melissa May

| $12 | 62 pages | 5.5" x 8.5" | softcover |

SparkleFat is a loud, unapologetic, intentional book of poetry about my body, about your body, about fat bodies and how they move through the world in every bit of their flash and spark and burst. Some of the poems are painful, some are raucous celebrations, some are reminders and love letters and quiet gifts back to the vessel that has traveled me so gracefully - some are a hymnal of yes, but all of them sparkle. All of them don't mind if you look – really. They built their own house of intention, and they draped that shit in lime green sequins. All of them intend to be seen.

All of them have no more fucks to give
about a world that wants them to be quiet.

Other titles available from
WORDS DANCE PUBLISHING

LOVE AND OTHER SMALL WARS

Poetry by Donna-Marie Riley

| $12 | 76 pages | 5.5" x 8.5" | softcover |

ISBN: 978-0615931111

Love and Other Small Wars reminds us that when you come back from combat usually the most fatal of wounds are not visible. Riley's debut collection is an arsenal of deeply personal poems that embody an intensity that is truly impressive yet their hands are tender. She enlists you. She gives you camouflage & a pair of boots so you can stay the course through the minefield of her heart. You will track the lovely flow of her soft yet fierce voice through a jungle of powerful imagery on womanhood, relationships, family, grief, sexuality & love, amidst other matters. Battles with the heart aren't easily won but Riley hits every mark. You'll be relieved that you're on the same side. Much like war, you'll come back from this book changed.

"Riley's work is wise, intense, affecting, and uniquely crafted. This collection illuminates her ability to write with both a gentle hand and a bold spirit. She inspires her readers and creates an indelible need inside of them to consume more of her exceptional poetry. I could read *Love and Other Small Wars* all day long…and I did."

— **APRIL MICHELLE BRATTEN**
editor of *Up the Staircase Quarterly*

"Riley's poems are personal, lyrical and so vibrant they practically leap off the page, which also makes them terrifying at times. A beautiful debut."

— **BIANCA STEWART**

Tammy Foster Brewer is the type of poet who makes me wish I could write poetry instead of novels. From motherhood to love to work, Tammy's poems highlight the extraordinary in the ordinary and leave the reader wondering how he did not notice what was underneath all along. I first heard Tammy read 'The Problem is with Semantics' months ago, and it's stayed with me ever since. Now that I've read the entire collection, I only hope I can make room to keep every one of her poems in my heart and mind tomorrow and beyond.

— **NICOLE ROSS**, author

NO GLASS ALLOWED
Poetry by Tammy Foster Brewer

$12 | 56 pages | 6" x 9" | softcover | ISBN: 978-0615870007

Brewer's collection is filled with uncanny details that readers will wear like the accessories of womanhood. Fishing the Chattahoochee, sideways trees, pollen on a car, white dresses and breast milk, and so much more -- all parts of a deeply intellectual pondering of what is often painful and human regarding the other halves of mothers and daughters, husbands and wives, lovers and lost lovers, children and parents.

— **NICHOLAS BELARDES**
author of *Songs of the Glue Machines*

Tammy deftly juxtaposes distinct imagery with stories that seem to collide in her brilliant poetic mind. Stories of transmissions and trees and the words we utter, or don't. Of floods and forgiveness, conversations and car lanes, bread and beginnings, awe and expectations, desire and leaps of faith that leave one breathless, and renewed.

"When I say I am a poet / I mean my house has many windows" has to be one of the best descriptions of what it's like to be a contemporary female poet who not only holds down a day job and raises a family, but whose mind and heart regularly file away fleeting images and ideas that might later be woven into something permanent, and perhaps even beautiful. This ability is not easily acquired. It takes effort, and time, and the type of determination only some writers, like Tammy, possess and are willing to actively exercise.

— **KAREN DEGROOT CARTER**
author of *One Sister's Song*

Unrequited love? We've all been there.

Enter:

WHAT TO DO AFTER SHE SAYS NO
by Kris Ryan.

This skillfully designed 10-part poem explores what it's like to ache for someone. This is the book you buy yourself or a friend when you are going through a breakup or a one-sided crush, it's the perfect balance between aha, humor & heartbreak.

WHAT TO DO AFTER SHE SAYS NO
A Poem by Kris Ryan

$10 | 104 pages | 5" x 8" | softcover | ISBN: 978-0615870045

"*What to Do After She Says No* takes us from Shanghai to the interior of a refrigerator, but mostly dwells inside the injured human heart, exploring the aftermath of emotional betrayal. This poem is a compact blast of brutality, with such instructions as "Climb onto the roof and jump off. If you break your leg, you are awake. If you land without injury, pinch and twist at your arm until you wake up." Ryan's use of the imperative often leads us to a reality where pain is the only outcome, but this piece is not without tenderness, and certainly not without play, with sounds and images ricocheting off each other throughout. Anticipate the poetry you wish you knew about during your last bad breakup; this poem offers a first "foothold to climb out" from that universal experience."

— **LISA MANGINI**

"Reading Kris Ryan's *What To Do After She Says No* is like watching your heart pound outside of your chest. Both an unsettling visual experience and a hurricane of sadness and rebirth—this book demands more than just your attention, it takes a little bit of your soul, and in the end, makes everything feel whole again."

— **JOHN DORSEY**
author of ***Tombstone Factory***

"*What to Do After She Says No* is exquisite. Truly, perfectly exquisite. It pulls you in on a familiar and wild ride of a heart blown open and a mind twisting in an effort to figure it all out. It's raw and vibrant...and in the same breath comforting. I want to crawl inside this book and live in a world where heartache is expressed so magnificently.

— **JO ANNA ROTHMAN**
MA, Coach & Conjurer of Electric Creative Wholeness

WORDS DANCE PUBLISHING has one aim:

To spread mind-blowing / heart-opening poetry.

Words Dance artfully & carefully wrangles words that were born to dance wildly in the heart-mind matrix. Rich, edgy, raw, emotionally-charged energy balled up & waiting to whip your eyes wild; we rally together words that were written to make your heart go boom right before they slay your mind. You dig?

Words Dance Publishing is an independent press out of Pennsylvania. We work closely & collaboratively with all of our writers to ensure that their words continue to breathe in a sound & stunning home. Most importantly though, we leave the windows in these homes unlocked so you, the reader, can crawl in & throw one fuck of a house party.

To learn more about our books, authors, events & Words Dance Poetry Magazine, visit:

WORDSDANCE.COM

Printed in Great Britain
by Amazon